AF351108

GUIDE BOOK FOR BUSINESS ORGANIZATION AS PER BODOLAND UNIVERSITY SYLLABUS

B.COM: SEMESTER – I (PART-A)

ANJOY BASUMATARY | M.COM | NET | SLET

Contents

Preface

"Welcome to this comprehensive guidebook on Business Organization. This guidebook is designed to be a valuable resource for B.COM students who are looking as a comprehensive reference book as per Bodoland University Syllabus.

Throughout the book, you will find questions and answers that will help you cover the entire syllabus. The book is organized in a systematic manner as per the syllabus published by Bodoland University, so that you can easily find the information you need.

I hope that this guidebook will be a valuable resource for you as you prepare for the exams. If you have any further questions or need additional help, please feel free to my mail as anjoybasumatary@ustm.ac.in

Thank you for choosing this guidebook. I hope that it helps you achieve your goals and that you find it to be a valuable resource."

Please let me know if there's something specific you would like to include or if there's anything else I can help you with.

1. What is Business Organisation? What are the different types of Business Organisation?

Ans: Business organization refers to the structure and design of a business and how it operates. It includes the formal and informal systems, processes, and protocols that are put in place to manage the various tasks and responsibilities of the organization. This can include the type of legal structure of the business, the roles and responsibilities of employees and management, the decision-making processes, and the overall culture and values of the organization. The form of organization chosen will have legal and financial implications and will depend on the type of business, size, and management style.

There are several forms of business organization, including:

1. Sole proprietorship: A business owned and operated by one person.
2. Partnership: A business owned and operated by two or more people.
3. Corporation: A business that is a separate legal entity from its owners, allowing them to limit their personal liability for the company's debts or lawsuits.
4. Limited Liability Company (LLC): A hybrid type of legal structure that provides the limited liability features of a corporation and the tax benefits of a partnership.
5. Cooperative: A business owned and controlled by the people who use its services or products.
6. Non-profit organization: A business that is organized for a specific purpose other than making a profit.

2. What are the advantage and disadvantages of Business Organisation?

Ans: There are several advantages to having a well-organized business, including:

1. **Increased efficiency:** A well-organized business will have clear systems and processes in place, which can lead to increased efficiency and productivity.

2. **Better decision-making:** A well-structured organization will have clear lines of authority and decision-making processes, which can help ensure that decisions are made in a timely and effective manner.

3. **Improved communication:** A well-organized business will have clear communication channels in place, which can help improve the flow of information and reduce misunderstandings.

4. **Greater accountability:** A well-organized business will have clear roles and responsibilities for employees, which can help ensure that everyone is accountable for their actions.

5. **Better financial management:** A well-organized business will have clear financial systems in place, which can help ensure that the business is financially stable and profitable.

6. **Better risk management:** A well-organized business will have clear systems and processes in place for identifying and managing risks, which can help protect the business from potential threats.

7. **Better adaptation:** A well-organized business is capable of adapting to the changes in the environment and the market.

8. **Increased chances of success:** A well-organized business is more likely to be successful as it has clear goals, objectives, and plans in place to achieve them.

While there are many advantages to having a well-organized business, there are also some potential disadvantages, including:

1. **Bureaucracy:** A well-organized business may have many rules and procedures in place, which can lead to bureaucracy and slow down decision-making and problem-solving.

2. **Loss of flexibility:** A well-organized business may have strict systems and processes in place, which can limit the flexibility of the organization to respond quickly to changes in the market or environment.

3. **Increased costs:** Setting up and maintaining a well-organized business can be costly, including legal fees for setting up the appropriate legal structure, and costs for creating and implementing systems and processes.

4. **Limited creativity:** A well-organized business may have strict rules and procedures in place, which can limit the creativity and innovation of employees.

5. **Dependence on key employees:** A well-organized business may rely heavily on key employees for decision-making and problem-solving, which can be problematic if those employees leave the company.
6. **Inflexibility:** A well-organized business may find it hard to adapt to the changes in the market or the environment.
7. **Stagnation:** A well-organized business may become stagnant if it does not adapt to the changing market conditions.
8. **Resistance to change:** A well-organized business may face resistance from employees to change the established systems and processes.

In summary, it's important to find a balance between the need for organization and the need for flexibility in order to maximize the chances of success of a business.

3. What is Multi-National Corporation (MNC)?

Ans: A Multinational Corporation (MNC) is a business entity that operates in multiple countries, with a centralized management structure and a global approach to production and marketing. MNCs typically have a parent company and subsidiaries or branches in other countries. They tend to be large, diversified companies with the resources and capabilities to operate on a global scale. They are involved in a wide range of industries, such as manufacturing, finance, retail, technology, and services.

MNCs often have a significant economic and political influence in the countries in which they operate. They can create jobs, drive economic growth, and bring new technologies and products to market. However, they can also face criticism for their business practices, such as exploiting workers or engaging in tax avoidance.

MNCs can be beneficial for the host countries by providing jobs, technology and investment. However, they can also be negative by exploiting natural resources, creating a negative impact on the environment, and engaging in unethical business practices.

4. What are the features of MNCs?

Ans: The main features of multinational corporations (MNCs) are:

1. **Global operations:** MNCs operate in multiple countries, with a centralized management structure and a global approach to production and marketing.
2. **Diversified businesses:** MNCs tend to be large, diversified companies with the resources and capabilities to operate on a global scale. They are

involved in a wide range of industries, such as manufacturing, finance, retail, technology, and services.

3. **Centralized management:** MNCs have a parent company and subsidiaries or branches in other countries. The parent company typically has overall control and decision-making authority for the entire organization.

4. **Economies of scale:** MNCs can take advantage of economies of scale by producing goods and services on a large scale and spreading fixed costs over a larger number of units.

5. **Brand recognition:** MNCs often have strong brand recognition, which can give them a competitive advantage in the global market.

6. **Advanced technology:** MNCs often have the resources to invest in advanced technology, which can give them a competitive advantage in terms of production efficiency and product quality.

7. **Financial resources:** MNCs typically have significant financial resources, which allows them to invest in research and development, expansion, and acquisitions.

8. **Political influence:** MNCs often have significant economic and political influence in the countries in which they operate.

9. **Ethical concerns:** MNCs can face criticism for their business practices, such as exploiting workers or engaging in tax avoidance.

10. **Global impact:** MNCs can have a significant impact on the global economy and can shape the business environment in the countries where they operate.

5. What are the different types of MNCs?

Ans: There are several forms of multinational corporations (MNCs), including:

1. **The Multidomestic Corporation:** This type of MNC operates in multiple countries, but each country is treated as a separate market, with a separate business strategy and operations. They tend to tailor their products and services to meet the specific needs and preferences of each local market.

2. **The Global Corporation:** This type of MNC operates in multiple countries with a centralized management structure and a global approach to production and marketing. They tend to standardize products, processes and management practices across all their

operations.

3. **The Transnational Corporation:** This type of MNC operates in multiple countries, with a decentralized management structure and a focus on balancing the needs of global efficiency with local responsiveness. They tend to seek a balance between global integration and local responsiveness, by combining elements of both multidomestic and global strategies.

4. **The International Corporation:** This type of MNC operates in multiple countries, but primarily exports goods and services from their home country to other countries. They tend to be focused on exporting their products and services to other countries, rather than adapting them to local markets.

5. **The Regional Corporation:** This type of MNC operates primarily in a specific region or group of countries, rather than globally. They tend to focus on a specific geographic region, rather than operating on a global scale.

6. **The State-Owned Corporation:** This type of MNC is owned, controlled, and operated by a government. They tend to be controlled and operated by a government, rather than by private investors.

It's worth noting that MNCs can evolve over time and may change their approach to global operations. Some may start as multidomestic and later become global or transnational, depending on their needs, goals, and the environment.

6. What are the advantages of MNCs?

Ans: There are several advantages of multinational corporations (MNCs) including:

1. **Economic growth:** MNCs can create jobs, drive economic growth, and bring new technologies and products to market.

2. **Increased efficiency:** MNCs can take advantage of economies of scale by producing goods and services on a large scale and spreading fixed costs over a larger number of units.

3. **Access to new markets:** MNCs can expand their operations to new markets, increasing their customer base and revenue potential.

4. **Brand recognition:** MNCs often have strong brand recognition, which can give them a competitive advantage in the global market.

5. **Advanced technology:** MNCs often have the resources to invest in advanced technology, which can give them a competitive advantage in terms of production efficiency and product quality.
6. **Financial resources:** MNCs typically have significant financial resources, which allows them to invest in research and development, expansion, and acquisitions.
7. **Global impact:** MNCs can have a significant impact on the global economy and can shape the business environment in the countries where they operate.
8. **Improved living standards:** MNCs can bring advanced technology, better working conditions, and higher wages, which can improve the living standards of the people in the host countries.
9. **Cultural exchange:** MNCs can promote cultural exchange and understanding by exposing people in different countries to different ways of life and different perspectives.
10. **Greater competition:** MNCs can increase competition in the global market, which can lead to lower prices and better products for consumers.

7. What are the limitations of MNCs?

Ans: While there are many advantages to multinational corporations (MNCs), there are also some potential limitations, including:

1. **Exploitation of resources:** MNCs may exploit natural resources in host countries for their own gain, without regard for the local people or the environment.
2. **Negative impact on the environment:** MNCs may engage in practices that have a negative impact on the environment, such as pollution and deforestation.
3. **Unfair labor practices:** MNCs may exploit workers in host countries by paying low wages and providing poor working conditions.
4. **Cultural imperialism:** MNCs may impose their own cultural values and practices on host countries, leading to the erosion of local traditions and customs.
5. **Dependence on MNCs:** Host countries may become too dependent on MNCs, which can lead to a lack of diversity in the economy and make them vulnerable to economic downturns.

6. **Tax avoidance:** MNCs may engage in tax avoidance by transferring profits to subsidiaries in countries with lower tax rates.

7. **Competition with local businesses:** MNCs may compete with and drive out local businesses, leading to a loss of jobs and economic decline in host countries.

8. **Limited accountability:** MNCs may be able to operate with limited accountability, as they may be able to influence government policies and regulations in host countries.

9. **Lack of transparency:** MNCs may lack transparency in their operations, which can make it difficult for host countries to monitor and regulate their activities.

10. **Political influence:** MNCs may have significant political influence in host countries, which can lead to corruption and abuse of power.

8. What is Joint Sector?

Ans: Joint sector refers to a form of business organization in which the government and private sector companies collaborate to establish and operate a business venture. In a joint sector venture, the government and private companies share the ownership, management and control of the business. The government usually provides the land and other infrastructure, while the private companies provide the capital, technology, and management expertise.

The joint sector can take various forms, such as joint ventures, public-private partnerships (PPP), or government-owned corporations. The main objective of the joint sector is to combine the strengths of the government and private sector to achieve a common goal, such as promoting economic development, improving infrastructure, or providing essential services to the public. Joint sector can be beneficial for both parties, as it allows the government to leverage private sector resources and expertise to achieve public policy goals, while private companies can benefit from the government's resources, such as land and infrastructure. However, joint sector can also face challenges, such as lack of transparency, lack of accountability, and difficulties in coordinating the different interests of the parties involved.

9. What are the features of Joint Sector?

Ans: The main features of joint sector are:

1. **Collaboration between government and private sector:** Joint sector is a form of business organization in which the government and private companies work together to establish and operate a business venture.
2. **Shared ownership:** In a joint sector venture, the government and private companies share ownership, management and control of the business.
3. **Different resource contribution:** The government usually provides resources such as land, subsidies and other infrastructures, while the private sector provides capital, technology, and management expertise.
4. **Public-private partnership:** Joint sector is often established as a public-private partnership (PPP), where the government and private sector work together to provide services and infrastructure to the public.
5. **Various forms:** Joint sector can take various forms such as joint ventures, public-private partnerships (PPP), or government-owned corporations.
6. **Achieving common goals:** The main objective of the joint sector is to combine the strengths of the government and private sector to achieve a common goal, such as promoting economic development, improving infrastructure, or providing essential services to the public.
7. **Greater Efficiency:** By pooling resources, the joint sector can achieve greater efficiency than either sector working alone.
8. **Risk sharing:** Risk is shared between the government and private companies, which can help to mitigate the impact of potential losses or setbacks.
9. **Transparency and Accountability:** Joint sector ventures are often subject to greater transparency and accountability than solely government-run or privately-run ventures.
10. **Challenges:** Joint sector can also face challenges, such as lack of transparency, lack of accountability, and difficulties in coordinating the different interests of the parties involved.

10. What is the importance of Joint Sector?

Ans: Joint sector can be an important form of business organization as it allows the government and private sector to collaborate and leverage their respective strengths to achieve common goals. Some of the key benefits of joint sector include:

1. **Greater Efficiency:** By pooling resources, the joint sector can achieve greater efficiency than either sector working alone. This can lead to cost

savings, improved service delivery and better use of resources.

2. **Risk sharing:** Risk is shared between the government and private companies, which can help to mitigate the impact of potential losses or setbacks. This can make it easier for businesses to invest in infrastructure and other long-term projects.

3. **Improved infrastructure:** Joint sector can be used to improve infrastructure, such as building new highways, power plants, and water treatment facilities. This can lead to economic growth and improved living standards.

4. **Promotion of Economic Development:** Joint sector can be used to promote economic development in underdeveloped or remote areas by providing access to capital, technology, and management expertise.

5. **Job creation:** By creating new businesses and expanding existing ones, joint sector can create jobs and improve economic opportunities for people.

6. **Improved public services:** Joint sector can be used to improve public services, such as healthcare and education, by leveraging private sector expertise and resources.

7. **Transparency and Accountability:** Joint sector ventures are often subject to greater transparency and accountability than solely government-run or privately-run ventures.

8. **Flexibility:** Joint sector allows for more flexibility in addressing public policy objectives and can be adapted to changing circumstances.

9. **Encourage private investment:** Joint sector can encourage private investment in areas where the government alone would not be able to provide the necessary resources.

10. **Enhancing development:** Joint sector ventures can be an effective way to enhance the development of underdeveloped regions and can promote sustainable development.

11. Definition of Franchise?

Ans: A franchise is a type of business model in which the owner of a trademark, trade name, or product (the franchisor) grants the right to use that trademark, trade name, or product to another person or company (the franchisee) in exchange for an initial fee and ongoing royalties. The franchisee usually receives a package of goods or services from the franchisor, including training, support, and marketing materials. In return, the franchisee agrees to operate their business according to the franchisor's established systems and procedures, including the use of certain products, trademarks and marketing strategies.

Franchising is a popular form of business expansion, as it allows the franchisor to expand their brand and business quickly and efficiently, while also providing the franchisee with a proven business model, established customer base, and access to existing supply chains. However, franchisees often have to share a percentage of their revenues with the franchisor, and may also have to pay ongoing royalties and fees.

12. What the different types of Franchising?

Ans: There are several types of franchising, including:

1. **Product Distribution Franchising:** This type of franchising involves the distribution of a specific product or product line, such as a well-known brand of car parts or a line of clothing. The franchisee is typically responsible for marketing and selling the product, while the franchisor provides support and training.
2. **Business Format Franchising:** This is the most common type of franchising, it involves the use of a complete business model, including the use of a trademark, trade name, and established systems and procedures. The franchisee receives training and support from the franchisor, and is typically responsible for the day-to-day operations of the business.
3. **Management Franchising:** This type of franchising involves the franchisor providing management services to the franchisee, who is responsible for the day-to-day operations of the business. The franchisor is typically responsible for hiring and training employees, and may also be involved in other aspects of the business.
4. **Single-Unit Franchising:** This type of franchising involves one franchisee operating one business location.
5. **Multi-Unit Franchising:** This type of franchising involves one franchisee operating multiple business locations.
6. **Area Development Franchising:** This type of franchising involves a franchisee being granted the rights to develop a specific geographic area, and opening multiple units over time in that area.
7. **Master Franchising:** This type of franchising involves granting a franchisee the rights to sub-franchise within a specific geographic area.
8. **Online/Virtual Franchising:** This type of franchising allows the franchisee to operate a business online or remotely, with the franchisor

providing training and support, as well as a proven business model.

13. What are the Merits and Demerits of Franchising?
Ans: There are several advantages or merits of franchising, including:

1. **Proven Business Model:** Franchising provides the franchisee with a proven business model, established customer base, and access to existing supply chains, which can increase the chances of success for the franchisee.
2. **Brand Recognition:** A well-established franchisor can provide the franchisee with instant brand recognition, which can help to attract customers and increase visibility for the business.
3. **Training and Support:** Franchisors typically provide training and support to franchisees, which can help them to learn the business quickly and operate it effectively.
4. **Marketing and Advertising:** The franchisor typically provides marketing and advertising support to franchisees, which can help to promote the business and attract customers.
5. **Economies of Scale:** Franchisors can take advantage of economies of scale by purchasing goods and services in bulk, which can help to lower costs for the franchisee.
6. **Reduced Risk:** By purchasing a franchise, the franchisee can reduce the risk of starting a new business, as they are buying into an established brand and business model.
7. **Flexibility:** Franchisees can choose to operate the business full-time or part-time, depending on their personal circumstances and goals.
8. **Sharing of knowledge:** Franchisees can benefit from the knowledge and expertise of the franchisor, which can help them to improve their business operations and achieve better results.
9. **Continual improvement:** Franchisees can continuously improve their business by implementing new systems, processes, and best practices developed by the franchisor.
10. **Continuous Support:** Franchisees can receive ongoing support from the franchisor, which can help them to resolve issues and overcome challenges.

While franchising can be a successful business model, there are also some potential drawbacks or demerits to consider, including:

1. **Initial Costs:** The initial costs of purchasing a franchise can be high, including franchise fees, training expenses, and the cost of equipment and inventory.
2. **Ongoing Fees:** Franchisees may be required to pay ongoing royalties and fees to the franchisor, which can be a significant ongoing expense.
3. **Limited Control:** Franchisees may have limited control over how they run their business, as they must follow the franchisor's established systems and procedures.
4. **Limited Market:** Franchisees may be restricted to a specific geographic area or market, which can limit the potential for growth and expansion.
5. **Dependence on franchisor:** Franchisees may become too dependent on the franchisor for support and resources, which can make them vulnerable to changes in the franchisor's business.
6. **Limited autonomy:** Franchisees may have limited autonomy, as they may be bound by a strict set of rules and regulations set by the franchisor.
7. **Limited freedom:** Franchisees may have limited freedom to make changes to their business, such as changing pricing or product offerings.
8. **Limited negotiation power:** Franchisees may have limited negotiation power with suppliers, landlords, and other partners, as they may not be able to leverage the same economies of scale as the franchisor.
9. **Limited access to information:** Franchisees may have limited access to the franchisor's financial or other critical information.
10. **Limited ability to innovate:** Franchisees may have limited ability to innovate or adapt to changing market conditions as they are bound by the franchisor's established systems and procedures.

14. Definition of Enterprise? What is Micro-Enterprise?

Ans: An enterprise is a business organization, typically a company or firm, that engages in commercial, industrial, or professional activities. An enterprise can range in size from a small, one-person operation to a large multinational corporation. The term "enterprise" can refer to a wide range of business activities, including manufacturing, retail, services, and more. It is often used to describe a business venture that is focused on innovation, growth, and profitability. The term is also used to describe a specific project or initiative within a company, such as an enterprise resource planning (ERP) system or an enterprise-wide data analytics project.

A micro enterprise is a small business that typically has fewer than 10 employees and relatively low revenues. These businesses are often owned and operated by a single person or a small group of individuals, and may provide goods or services to consumers or other businesses. Micro enterprises are considered as the backbone of the economy and considered as the key drivers of economic growth and job creation in many developing countries. They are known for their flexibility, adaptability and ability to create jobs in areas where larger companies cannot. Some examples of micro enterprises include small retail shops, home-based businesses, and self-employed professionals such as plumbers, electricians, and hairdressers.

15. What is Medium Enterprise?

Ans: A medium enterprise, also known as a small and medium-sized enterprise (SME), is a business that typically has between 10 and 250 employees and relatively moderate revenues. They are considered as the key drivers of economic growth and job creation in many developed countries. These businesses can operate in a wide range of industries, including manufacturing, retail, services, and more. They are considered to have a more substantial infrastructure and resources than micro-enterprises and are capable of generating significant economic and social impact. Medium enterprises often have a higher turnover and more employees than micro enterprises, but they still remain small enough to be flexible and agile in their operations. They often have more specialized management teams and are more likely to have a broader range of products or services than micro enterprises. They are also more likely to have a more formalized organizational structure, and may have a board of directors or a management team that is responsible for the overall direction of the company.

16. What is the concept of Virtual and Learning Organisation?

Ans: A virtual organization is a type of business structure that allows employees to work remotely and communicate primarily through technology, such as email, video conferencing, and instant messaging. Virtual organizations have no physical office space, and employees may be located in different geographic locations. They leverage technology to enable collaboration and communication among employees.

A learning organization is an organization that continuously seeks to improve its processes and performance through a culture of learning and development. This concept was first introduced by Peter Senge in his book

"The Fifth Discipline: The Art and Practice of the Learning Organization". A learning organization is one that is constantly looking for ways to improve, and encourages employees to take risks and experiment with new ideas. They are characterized by a culture of continuous learning, where employees are encouraged to learn from their mistakes and to share their knowledge and experience with others.

Both the concept of virtual organization and learning organization have been gaining popularity in recent years, particularly with advancements in technology that make it easier to work remotely and stay connected with others. Companies that adopt these concepts are able to gain a competitive advantage by leveraging the latest technology to improve communication and collaboration, while also building a culture of learning and development that can help them to continuously improve and innovate.

CHAPTER II

1. What do you mean Business Combinations?

Ans: Business combinations, also known as mergers and acquisitions (M&A), refer to the process of combining two or more businesses into one. This can be done through a merger, where two or more companies combine to form a new entity, or an acquisition, where one company buys or takes control of another company. Business combinations can take place between companies of similar sizes and in the same industry, or between companies of vastly different sizes and in different industries.

There are several reasons why companies engage in business combinations, including:

1. **Market dominance:** Combining with or acquiring a competitor can help a company to increase its market share and gain a competitive advantage.
2. **Economies of scale:** Combining resources and operations can lead to cost savings and increased efficiency.
3. **Diversification:** Acquiring a company in a different industry can help to diversify a company's revenue streams and mitigate risk.
4. **Synergy:** Combining two companies can lead to the creation of new revenue streams and the ability to offer new products or services.
5. **Access to new technology or talent:** Acquiring a company can give a company access to new technology or a talented workforce that it may not have had access to before.

However, not all business combinations are successful, and it is important to consider the potential risks and challenges that can arise during the process, such as cultural clashes, integration issues, and regulatory hurdles.

2. What are the causes of Business Combinations?

Ans: There are several causes of business combinations, including:

1. **Market growth:** Companies may seek to expand their market share and capitalize on growth opportunities by acquiring or merging with other companies.

2. **Increased competitiveness:** Companies may seek to increase their competitiveness by acquiring or merging with companies that have complementary products, services, or technologies.

3. **Diversification:** Companies may seek to diversify their revenue streams and reduce their overall risk by acquiring or merging with companies in different industries or markets.

4. **Cost savings:** Companies may seek to achieve cost savings through economies of scale by merging with or acquiring other companies.

5. **Access to new resources:** Companies may seek to acquire or merge with other companies to gain access to new resources such as technology, talent, or intellectual property.

6. **Tax benefits:** Companies may seek to acquire or merge with other companies to take advantage of tax benefits such as lower tax rates or tax deductions.

7. **Financial stability:** Companies may seek to acquire or merge with other companies to improve their financial stability and secure their long-term growth.

8. **Strategic positioning:** Companies may seek to acquire or merge with other companies in order to improve their strategic position in the market, such as by gaining a stronger foothold in a particular geographic region or industry.

These are some of the causes that drive companies to engage in business combinations, but they may vary depending on the specific circumstances of each case.

3. What are the types of Mergers of Business Organisations?

Ans: There are several types of mergers, each with its own set of characteristics and implications:

1. **Horizontal merger:** A merger between two companies that operate in the same industry and at the same stage of the production process. This type of merger can increase market share, eliminate competition and achieve economies of scale.

2. **Vertical merger:** A merger between two companies that operate at different stages of the production process. This type of merger can increase control over the supply chain and reduce dependency on suppliers or customers.

3. **Conglomerate merger:** A merger between two companies that operate in completely different industries. This type of merger can diversify a company's revenue streams and mitigate risk.

4. **Market-extension merger:** A merger between two companies that operate in the same industry but in different geographic markets. This type of merger can increase market share and achieve economies of scale.

5. **Product-extension merger:** A merger between two companies that operate in the same industry and geographic market but offer different products. This type of merger can increase product offerings and achieve economies of scale.

6. **Reverse merger:** A merger in which a private company is acquired by a publicly traded company. This type of merger can provide a private company with access to public markets and capital.

7. **Consolidation merger:** A merger between several companies in the same industry, with the goal of creating a larger, more dominant market player. This type of merger can increase market share and achieve economies of scale.

8. **Reverse triangular merger:** A merger in which the acquiring company forms a new subsidiary to acquire the target company, in which the target company's shareholders receive stock in the new subsidiary rather than cash or stock in the acquiring company.

The choice of merger type depends on the companies' objectives, strategies and the industry they operate in.

4. What are the different forms of Merger?

Ans: There are several forms of mergers of business, each with its own set of characteristics and implications:

1. **Statutory merger:** A merger in which one company (the surviving company) absorbs the assets and liabilities of another company (the merging company) and continues as a single entity.

2. **Consolidation merger:** A merger in which two or more companies combine to form a new entity.

3. **Stock merger:** A merger in which the shareholders of the merging company receive stock in the surviving company in exchange for their shares.

4. **Cash merger:** A merger in which the shareholders of the merging company receive cash in exchange for their shares.

5. **Asset merger:** A merger in which the assets of the merging company are transferred to the surviving company in exchange for cash, stock, or other assets.

6. **Reverse merger:** A merger in which a private company is acquired by a publicly traded company, in which the private company's shareholders receive stock in the publicly traded company in exchange for their shares.

7. **Triangular merger:** A merger in which a target company is acquired by a subsidiary of the acquiring company, rather than by the acquiring company directly.

8. **Reverse triangular merger:** A merger in which the acquiring company forms a new subsidiary to acquire the target company, in which the target company's shareholders receive stock in the new subsidiary rather than cash or stock in the acquiring company.

9. **Recapitalization:** A merger in which one company's shareholders exchange their shares for shares of another company.

10. **Management buyout (MBO):** A merger in which the management team of a company buys out the company from its existing shareholders.

11. **Leveraged buyout (LBO):** A merger in which a company is acquired through the use of significant amounts of debt, with the assets of the company serving as collateral for the loans.

The choice of merger form depends on the companies' objectives, strategies, and financial situations, as well as the industry they operate in, and the legal and regulatory environment they are operating in.

5. What are the Merger and Acquisition policies in India?

Ans: In India, merger and acquisition (M&A) activity is regulated by the Competition Commission of India (CCI) and the Securities and Exchange Board of India (SEBI). The CCI is responsible for ensuring that M&A deals do not lead to a reduction of competition in the market, while SEBI regulates securities markets and protects the interests of investors.

The Indian government has set up the Foreign Investment Promotion Board (FIPB) to process and approve foreign investment proposals. The FIPB examines each proposal on a case-by-case basis, taking into account factors such as the impact on the domestic industry and the country's foreign exchange reserves.

The Indian government has also introduced several policies to encourage M&A activity in the country, including:

1. Liberalization of foreign investment rules: The government has relaxed restrictions on foreign investment in several sectors, such as retail, insurance, and telecommunications, to make it easier for foreign companies to invest in India.
2. Simplified merger procedures: The government has made the merger process simpler and faster by introducing a one-stop clearance system and reducing the time required for approvals.
3. Sector-specific policies: The government has introduced sector-specific policies, such as the "Make in India" initiative, to promote investment and growth in certain sectors.
4. Tax incentives: The government has introduced tax incentives to encourage M&A activity in the country.
5. Ease of Doing Business: The Government of India has initiated several measures to improve the ease of doing business in the country, which includes the merger and acquisition process.
6. National Company Law Tribunal (NCLT) : The NCLT has been set up to fast-track the merger and acquisition process by providing a single-window clearance for all regulatory approvals.

However, despite these policies, M&A activity in India has been relatively slow due to some of the challenges such as high debt levels, lack of transparency and weak corporate governance. Furthermore, the compliance with various laws and regulations can be complex and time-consuming, creating additional obstacles for M&A activity.

6. What are the steps involved in setting up a new enterprise?

Ans: Setting up a new enterprise involves several steps, including:

1. **Business Idea:** Develop a clear and well-defined business idea, conduct market research, and identify the target audience and the competition.
2. **Business Plan:** Prepare a comprehensive business plan, including details of the product or service, marketing strategy, financial projections, and organizational structure.
3. **Legal Structure:** Choose the appropriate legal structure for the business, such as sole proprietorship, partnership, limited liability company (LLC) or corporation.

4. **Financing:** Secure financing for the business, which can include equity investment, debt financing, or a combination of both.
5. **Business registration:** Register the business with the relevant government authorities, including registering the company name, obtaining a PAN and TAN number, registering for GST and obtaining a trade license.
6. **Obtain necessary licenses and permits:** Obtain any necessary licenses and permits required to operate the business, such as business licenses, tax identification numbers, and zoning permits.
7. **Location and infrastructure:** Identify and secure a suitable location for the business, and set up the necessary infrastructure to support operations.
8. **Hiring employees:** Hire employees as needed, ensure compliance with labor laws, and provide necessary training.
9. **IT and technology:** Establish an IT infrastructure and acquire necessary technology to support business operations.
10. **Operations:** Develop and implement systems and procedures for daily operations, such as inventory management, accounting, and customer service.
11. **Marketing and promotion:** Develop a marketing and promotion strategy to attract customers and promote the business.
12. **Compliance:** Ensure compliance with all relevant laws and regulations, such as labor laws, tax laws, and environmental laws.

Keep in mind that regulations and requirements for setting up a business can vary depending on the location and industry. It's important to consult with legal and financial professionals to ensure compliance with all laws and regulations.

7. What do you mean by site selection and location theories according to Max Weber & Sargent Florence theories?

Ans: Site selection and location theories refer to the process of selecting the best location for a business or organization to operate. The selection of the right location can have a significant impact on the success of a business.

Max Weber's theory of industrial location, also known as Weber's theory of location, is one of the earliest and most influential theories on the subject of site selection. Weber argued that businesses tend to locate near sources of raw materials and transportation infrastructure, in order to minimize production costs. He believed that the location decision was based on cost-minimization, where firms would seek to minimize the costs of inputs, such as labor and raw materials. He also suggested that businesses will tend to locate near other businesses that are involved in similar industries, in order to take advantage of economies of scale and shared resources.

Sargent Florence's theory of interregional trade, also known as the theory of industrial location, built upon Weber's theory by suggesting that businesses will tend to locate near other businesses that are involved in similar industries, in order to take advantage of economies of scale and shared resources. Florence also added that businesses will tend to locate near areas that have a strong economic base, such as a large population, a well-educated workforce, or a strong infrastructure. He emphasized on the importance of the market access in the location decision, where firms would choose a location that would enable them to access their target market with ease.

Both of these theories are considered important contributions to the field of location theory and are still widely referenced today. However, it's worth noting that the theories have evolved over time with new research and technology. For example, transportation and communication technologies have a significant impact on the location decision making process which was not considered in the original theories. Furthermore, the availability of skilled labor and government policies also play an important role in the location decision making process.

8. What do you mean by size of a Business Unit?

Ans: The size of a business unit can refer to the number of employees, revenue, assets, or any other measure of the scale of a business. The size of a business unit can vary greatly, from small, locally-owned businesses with a few employees to large multinational corporations with thousands of employees and billions of dollars in revenue.

The size of a business unit can have a significant impact on the way it operates and the strategies it employs. For example, small business units may have a more flexible and agile organizational structure, while large business units may have a more bureaucratic structure with multiple layers of management.

Small business units may have limited resources, and may rely on personal relationships with customers and suppliers, while large business units may have more resources and may rely on more formalized business processes.

Smaller business units may be more vulnerable to market fluctuations, while larger business units may have more resources to weather economic downturns. Furthermore, smaller business units may have a more limited range of products or services and a small customer base, while larger business units may have a more diversified product or service offering and a larger customer base.

Size can also have an impact on the ability of a business to take on debt, raise capital, and make strategic acquisitions. Smaller business units may have more limited access to capital, while larger business units may have more resources to fund growth and expansion.

Additionally, the size of a business unit also affects the level of government regulations and compliance it needs to adhere to. Smaller business units may have fewer regulations to comply with, while larger business units may have more extensive regulatory requirements.

In summary, the size of a business unit can impact the business operations, the strategies that it employs, and the resources available to it. Businesses must consider their size and resources when developing strategies and making decisions.

9. Define the concept of Optimum firm?

Ans: An optimum firm refers to a business that has achieved the ideal balance between size, efficiency, and profitability. It is a firm that has reached the most efficient and profitable size for its industry, market, and resources.

An optimum firm is able to achieve the most efficient use of its resources by maximizing output while minimizing costs. It is able to produce the highest quality products or services at the lowest possible cost.

An optimum firm is able to achieve the ideal balance between size and efficiency by finding the most efficient scale of production. For example, a small firm may be more efficient in terms of labor costs but may not have the economies of scale that a larger firm would have.

In addition, an optimum firm is able to achieve the ideal balance between size and profitability. It is able to generate enough revenue to cover its costs and generate a profit, while also being able to invest in growth and expansion.

An optimum firm is also able to achieve the ideal balance between size and risk. It is able to take on the right level of risk to generate returns while also being able to manage the potential downside.

In practice, the concept of optimum firm is difficult to define and measure. It's a relative concept that varies depending on the industry and market conditions. The concept of optimum firm can also change over time as market conditions change and resources evolve.

10. What are the factors affecting the survival of small businesses?

Ans: There are several factors that can affect the survival of small businesses, including:

1. **Industry:** The industry in which a small business operates can play a significant role in its survival. Businesses in some industries, such as technology or healthcare, may have a higher chance of survival than those in other industries, such as retail or hospitality, which have been hit hard by the pandemic.

2. **Business Model:** A sound business model can help ensure the survival of a small business. This includes having a clear understanding of the target market, a well-defined value proposition, and a sustainable revenue stream.

3. **Financing:** Access to financing is crucial for small businesses. Without adequate funding, they may struggle to cover operational costs and invest in growth.

4. **Competition:** The level of competition in a market can make it more difficult for small businesses to survive. In highly competitive markets, small businesses may need to differentiate themselves in order to stand out.

5. **Market conditions:** Economic conditions, such as recession or inflation, can have a significant impact on small businesses. They need to be able to adapt and change their strategies accordingly.

6. **Government regulations:** Government regulations can affect the survival of small businesses in different ways, for example, heavy taxes, compliance cost and so on.

7. **Digital Technologies:** Small businesses that are able to adapt to digital technologies and online platforms will have an advantage over those that do not, as these technologies can help them reach more customers and increase their visibility.

8. **Management:** The leadership and management of a small business can also play a key role in its survival. Strong leaders are able to make strategic decisions and navigate challenges that arise.

All these factors can be interrelated and can affect small business survival in different ways.

CHAPTER III

1. Definition of Production Management?

Ans: Production management refers to the process of planning, organizing, directing, and controlling the resources (such as labor, materials, and equipment) needed to produce goods or services. It encompasses all aspects of the production process, from product design and development to sourcing materials and managing the production schedule. The goal of production management is to efficiently and effectively produce goods or services that meet the needs of customers while minimizing costs and maximizing profits.

Production management includes several key functions, such as:

1. **Planning:** This involves setting production goals and determining the resources needed to achieve them.
2. **Organizing:** This includes arranging the production process, including the layout of the production facility and the assignment of tasks to workers.
3. **Directing:** This involves providing guidance and supervision to workers to ensure that production goals are met.
4. **Controlling:** This includes monitoring the production process and making adjustments as needed to keep it running smoothly.
5. **Quality control:** This is the process of ensuring that the products or services produced meet a certain level of quality standards and customer requirements.
6. **Inventory management:** This is the process of managing the inventory of raw materials and finished goods, including forecasting demand, ordering and receiving materials and controlling inventory levels.

Production management can be applied to both manufacturing and service industries. It is important to note that production management is closely linked with other functions such as marketing, finance, and operations management and it's critical for the overall success of an organization.

2. What is the Scope of Production Management?

Ans: The scope of production management includes several key areas, which include:

1. **Product design and development:** This involves creating new products or improving existing ones to meet customer needs and preferences.
2. **Process design and improvement:** This includes identifying and implementing efficient and cost-effective production processes.
3. **Equipment and facility management:** This includes the maintenance and upkeep of production equipment and facilities, as well as the design of production layouts.
4. **Inventory management:** This includes forecasting demand, ordering and receiving materials, and controlling inventory levels.
5. **Quality control:** This includes setting and enforcing quality standards, as well as implementing quality control procedures to ensure that products or services meet customer requirements.
6. **Scheduling and production planning:** This includes creating a production schedule, allocating resources and monitoring production progress.
7. **Supply chain management:** This includes managing relationships with suppliers, coordinating materials and logistics, and ensuring that goods or services are delivered on time.
8. **Cost control:** This includes managing production costs and identifying areas where costs can be reduced.
9. **Safety and environmental management:** This includes ensuring that production processes are safe for workers and the environment.
10. **Human resources management:** This includes recruiting, hiring and training employees, as well as managing employee performance.

Overall, the scope of production management is broad and encompasses various aspects of the production process, from product design and development to inventory management and cost control. It involves making decisions and managing resources to achieve the production goals and objectives, while ensuring customer satisfaction.

3. What are the steps involve in production planning process?

Ans: The production planning process typically involves the following steps:

1. **Sales forecasting:** This step involves estimating the demand for the company's products or services in the future. This information is used to determine the amount of resources that will be needed to meet that demand.

2. **Capacity planning:** This step involves determining the amount of resources (such as labor, materials, and equipment) that will be required to meet the forecasted demand.

3. **Master production scheduling:** This step involves creating a schedule that outlines when products or services will be produced and in what quantities. This schedule is based on the forecasted demand and the available resources.

4. **Material requirements planning:** This step involves determining the materials and components that will be needed to produce the goods or services outlined in the master production schedule.

5. **Inventory management:** This step involves managing the inventory of raw materials and finished goods, including forecasting demand, ordering and receiving materials, and controlling inventory levels

6. **Capacity scheduling:** This step involves allocating resources (such as labor, machines, and tools) to specific production tasks and ensuring that they will be available when they are needed.

7. **Production control:** This step involves monitoring the production process and making adjustments as needed to ensure that the production schedule is being followed and that resources are being used efficiently.

8. **Quality control:** This step includes setting and enforcing quality standards, as well as implementing quality control procedures to ensure that products or services meet customer requirements.

9. **Cost control:** This step includes managing production costs and identifying areas where costs can be reduced.

10. **Continuous improvement:** This step involves regularly reviewing the production process and looking for ways to improve it. This can include identifying and eliminating bottlenecks, reducing production lead times, and increasing efficiency.

It's important to note that the production planning process may vary depending on the industry and the nature of the product or service being produced. However, these steps provide a general overview of the key steps involved in production planning.

4. Define Quality Control?

Ans: Quality control (QC) is the process of inspecting, testing, and evaluating products or services to ensure that they meet a certain level of quality standards and customer requirements. The goal of quality control is to identify and correct defects or problems before they reach the customer. Quality control includes several key steps, such as:

1. **Establishing quality standards:** This involves determining what level of quality is acceptable for a product or service, and setting standards and specifications accordingly.
2. **Inspection and testing:** This step involves inspecting products or services at various stages of the production process and testing them to ensure that they meet the established quality standards.
3. **Identifying and correcting defects:** If defects or problems are identified during inspection or testing, they must be corrected before the product or service is released to the customer.
4. **Documentation and record-keeping:** This step involves maintaining detailed records of all quality control activities, including inspection results, test data, and corrective actions taken.
5. **Continuous improvement:** This step involves regularly reviewing and analyzing quality control data, looking for ways to improve the process, and implementing changes as needed.

Quality control can be applied to a wide range of industries and products, including manufacturing, healthcare, and service industries. It is a critical aspect of production management and helps ensure that products or services meet the needs and expectations of customers.

Quality control techniques can vary depending on the industry and the nature of the product or service. Some techniques include Statistical Process Control, Six Sigma, Total Quality Management, and ISO standards.

5. What do you mean by Productivity?

Ans: Productivity is a measure of how efficiently resources (such as labor, materials, and equipment) are used to produce goods or services. It is typically defined as the ratio of output to inputs. Productivity can be measured in various ways depending on the industry and the type of goods or services being produced. For example, in manufacturing, productivity can be measured by the number of units produced per hour of labor, while in services, productivity can be measured by the number of transactions or customer interactions per hour.

There are two main types of productivity:

Labor productivity: This measures the output of goods or services per unit of labor input. It is typically measured as the ratio of output to labor hours.

Total factor productivity (TFP): This measures the efficiency with which all inputs (such as labor, capital, and materials) are used to produce output. It is typically measured as the ratio of output to all inputs.

Increasing productivity is important for organizations as it can lead to increased profits, higher levels of output, and improved competitiveness. There are various ways to improve productivity, such as:

- Implementing new technologies or processes
- Improving efficiency and organization
- Investing in training and development
- Encouraging employee engagement and empowerment

It is important to note that productivity is a relative measure, and it can be affected by various internal and external factors such as technology, market conditions, economic cycles and so on. Therefore, it should be regularly monitored and analyzed to identify areas for improvement.

6. What are the factors influencing the productivity?

Ans: There are several factors that can influence productivity, including:

1. **Technology:** The availability and use of new technologies can improve productivity by automating tasks and increasing efficiency.
2. **Workforce:** A well-trained, motivated, and engaged workforce can improve productivity by increasing the quality and quantity of output.
3. **Organizational structure:** A well-designed organizational structure can improve communication, coordination and decision making, leading to increased productivity.
4. **Management practices:** Effective management practices, such as clear goals, regular performance evaluations, and continuous improvement, can lead to increased productivity.
5. **Work environment:** A comfortable and safe work environment can lead to increased productivity by reducing employee absenteeism and turnover.
6. **Capital investment:** Investing in new equipment, facilities and infrastructure can improve productivity by increasing capacity and

efficiency.

7. **Economic conditions:** Factors such as inflation, interest rates and exchange rates can affect productivity by increasing costs, reducing consumer demand and limiting access to credit.

8. **Government policies:** Government policies such as taxes, regulations, and subsidies can affect productivity by increasing or decreasing the costs of production.

9. **Market conditions:** Factors such as competition, consumer demand, and global trends can influence productivity by affecting the ability of firms to sell their products or services.

All these factors can have a direct or indirect effect on productivity and they are interrelated. Understanding these factors and how they interact is important to identify opportunities to improve productivity and make better decisions.

7. What are the causes of low Productivity?

Ans: There are several causes of low productivity, including:

1. **Lack of technology or outdated equipment:** Using outdated technology or equipment can lead to increased downtime, reduced efficiency, and lower quality output.

2. **Poorly trained workforce:** A workforce that is not properly trained or lacks the necessary skills to perform their jobs can lead to lower productivity.

3. **Inefficient organizational structure:** Poor communication, coordination, and decision-making processes can lead to low productivity.

4. **Management practices:** Poor management practices, such as unclear goals, lack of accountability, and lack of continuous improvement can lead to low productivity.

5. **Uncomfortable or unsafe work environment:** Poor working conditions, such as high noise levels, poor lighting, or lack of safety precautions can lead to low productivity and high absenteeism.

6. **Lack of investment:** Insufficient investment in equipment, facilities and infrastructure can lead to increased downtime, reduced efficiency, and lower capacity.

7. **Economic conditions:** Factors such as inflation, interest rates, and exchange rates can increase costs, reduce consumer demand and limit

access to credit, leading to low productivity.

8. **Government policies:** Government policies such as taxes, regulations, and subsidies can affect productivity by increasing or decreasing the costs of production.

9. **Market conditions:** Factors such as competition, consumer demand, and global trends can influence productivity by affecting the ability of firms to sell their products or services.

10. **Poor Time management:** Employees might be wasting time on unimportant tasks, procrastinating, or multitasking, leading to low productivity.

11. **Stress:** High levels of stress can lead to decreased focus, increased absenteeism, and lower productivity.

It's important to note that low productivity can be caused by a combination of factors, and it can have a significant impact on a company's bottom line. Identifying the causes of low productivity and taking steps to address them can help improve efficiency and increase profits.

8. What do you mean by Product Rationalization?

Ans: Product rationalization is the process of evaluating a company's product portfolio and making decisions to optimize it by eliminating, consolidating, or improving products. The goal of product rationalization is to focus on the products or product lines that are most profitable, or have the greatest potential for growth, while phasing out or consolidating those that are not performing well.

Product rationalization can include several key steps, such as:

1. **Product analysis:** This step involves evaluating each product or product line in terms of profitability, market potential, and alignment with the company's overall strategy.

2. **Portfolio optimization:** This step involves making decisions to eliminate, consolidate, or improve products based on the analysis.

3. **Implementation:** This step involves implementing the decisions made in the previous steps, which may include discontinuing certain products, merging product lines, or investing in new product development.

4. **Monitoring and evaluation:** This step involves monitoring the results of the product rationalization and making adjustments as needed.

Product rationalization can be beneficial for companies as it can help them focus their resources on the products that are most likely to drive growth and profitability, while reducing costs by phasing out or consolidating underperforming products. It can also help companies better align their product portfolio with their overall strategic goals and better respond to changes in the market.

9. What are the aims and objectives of Product Rationalization?

Ans: The main aims and objectives of product rationalization are to optimize a company's product portfolio by focusing on the products that are most profitable or have the greatest potential for growth, while phasing out or consolidating those that are not performing well. Some specific aims and objectives of product rationalization include:

1. **Improving profitability:** By focusing on the most profitable products or product lines, companies can improve their overall profitability.

2. **Aligning product portfolio with company strategy:** By eliminating or consolidating products that do not align with the company's overall strategy, companies can ensure that their product portfolio is aligned with their goals and objectives.

3. **Reducing costs:** By phasing out or consolidating underperforming products, companies can reduce costs associated with producing, marketing, and distributing those products.

4. **Improving customer service:** By focusing on the products that are most important to customers, companies can improve customer service by ensuring that they are able to meet customer needs and expectations.

5. **Responding to market changes:** By regularly reviewing and optimizing their product portfolio, companies can better respond to changes in the market, such as new technologies, changing customer needs and new competitors.

6. **Optimizing the use of resources:** By eliminating or consolidating products that are not performing well, companies can optimize the use of resources, such as production equipment, personnel, and materials.

7. **Enhancing Product Quality:** by focusing on key products, companies can invest more in product development, research, and quality control, thus enhancing the quality of their products.

Overall, product rationalization can help companies make better use of their resources, improve profitability, and better respond to market changes, by aligning their product portfolio with their overall strategic goals.

10. What are the benefits of Product Rationalization?

Ans: Product rationalization can offer several benefits to a company, including:

1. **Increased profitability:** By focusing on the most profitable products or product lines, companies can improve their overall profitability.
2. **Reduced Costs:** By phasing out or consolidating underperforming products, companies can reduce costs associated with producing, marketing, and distributing those products.
3. **Improved efficiency:** By consolidating or eliminating products, companies can make better use of their resources, increase efficiency, and reduce waste.
4. **Better alignment with company strategy:** By eliminating or consolidating products that do not align with the company's overall strategy, companies can ensure that their product portfolio is aligned with their goals and objectives.
5. **Improved customer service:** By focusing on the products that are most important to customers, companies can improve customer service by ensuring that they are able to meet customer needs and expectations.
6. **Increased flexibility:** By regularly reviewing and optimizing their product portfolio, companies can better respond to changes in the market, such as new technologies, changing customer needs, and new competitors.
7. **Enhanced Brand image:** By reducing the number of products and focusing on the key ones, companies can create a stronger brand image and easier to identify products.
8. **Increased innovation:** By freeing up resources, companies can invest more in product development, research, and quality control, thus enhancing the quality of their products and increase innovation.

Overall, product rationalization can help companies increase profitability, reduce costs, improve efficiency, better align their product portfolio with their strategy, and respond more effectively to changes in the market.

11. What are the limitations of Product Rationalization?

Ans: Product rationalization, while offering many potential benefits, also has some limitations that companies should be aware of:

1. **Loss of revenue:** By phasing out or consolidating products, companies may lose revenue from those products and may take time to find new revenue streams.
2. **Disruption of supply chain:** By consolidating or eliminating products, companies may disrupt their supply chain and may have to find new suppliers.
3. **Impact on employees:** By phasing out or consolidating products, companies may have to lay off employees or reassign them to different roles, which can lead to morale issues and potential loss of valuable employees.
4. **Impact on customers:** By phasing out or consolidating products, companies may have to discontinue products that customers have grown to rely on, which can lead to customer dissatisfaction and potential loss of business.
5. **Difficulty in predicting market changes:** It can be difficult for companies to predict changes in the market, and if they make the wrong decisions about which products to eliminate or consolidate, they may miss out on potential growth opportunities.
6. **Difficulty in evaluating products:** It can be challenging for companies to evaluate products based on their potential for growth, profitability, and alignment with company strategy, as these factors can be difficult to quantify.
7. **Resistance to change:** Companies may face resistance from employees, customers, or suppliers to changes in the product portfolio, which can make implementation more difficult.

It's important for companies to carefully consider the potential limitations of product rationalization and take steps to mitigate any negative impacts. They should also regularly monitor the results and make adjustments as needed.